Bible Story

Coloring Book

BARBOUR
PUBLISHING

ISBN 978-1-61626-934-0

Illustrations by Kathy Arbuckle.

Cover Illustrations: Dede Putra

Published by Barbour Publishing, Inc., P.O. Box 719, Uhrichsville, Ohio 44683, www.barbourbooks.com

Our mission is to publish and distribute inspirational products offering exceptional value and biblical encouragement to the masses.

Printed in the United States of America.
Quad Graphics, Fairfield, PA 17320; October 2012; D10003543

In the beginning. . . (Genesis 1)

The Garden of Eden (Genesis 2)

The temptation (Genesis 3)

Noah and the ark (Genesis 6–9)

The rainbow (Genesis 9)

The Tower of Babel (Genesis 11)

Abraham and Sarah (Genesis 12–18)

Lot's wife turns to salt (Genesis 19)

Jacob's ladder (Genesis 28)

Joseph is sold as a slave (Genesis 37)

Joseph interprets dreams (Genesis 40–41)

Joseph forgives his brothers (Genesis 42–45)

A princess finds baby Moses (Exodus 2)

Moses and the burning bush (Exodus 3)

The plagues and Passover (Exodus 7–12)

Parting the Red Sea (Exodus 14)

Manna from heaven (Exodus 16)

Moses and God speak on the mountain (Exodus 19–31)

The golden calf (Exodus 32)

The tablets of stone (Exodus 34)

The tabernacle (Exodus 35–40)

Spies go into Canaan (Numbers 13)

Balaam and his donkey (Numbers 22)

Moses' last sermon (Deuteronomy)

The Jordan River parts (Joshua 3)

The Battle of Jericho (Joshua 6)

The lamps and trumpets of Gideon (Judges 7)

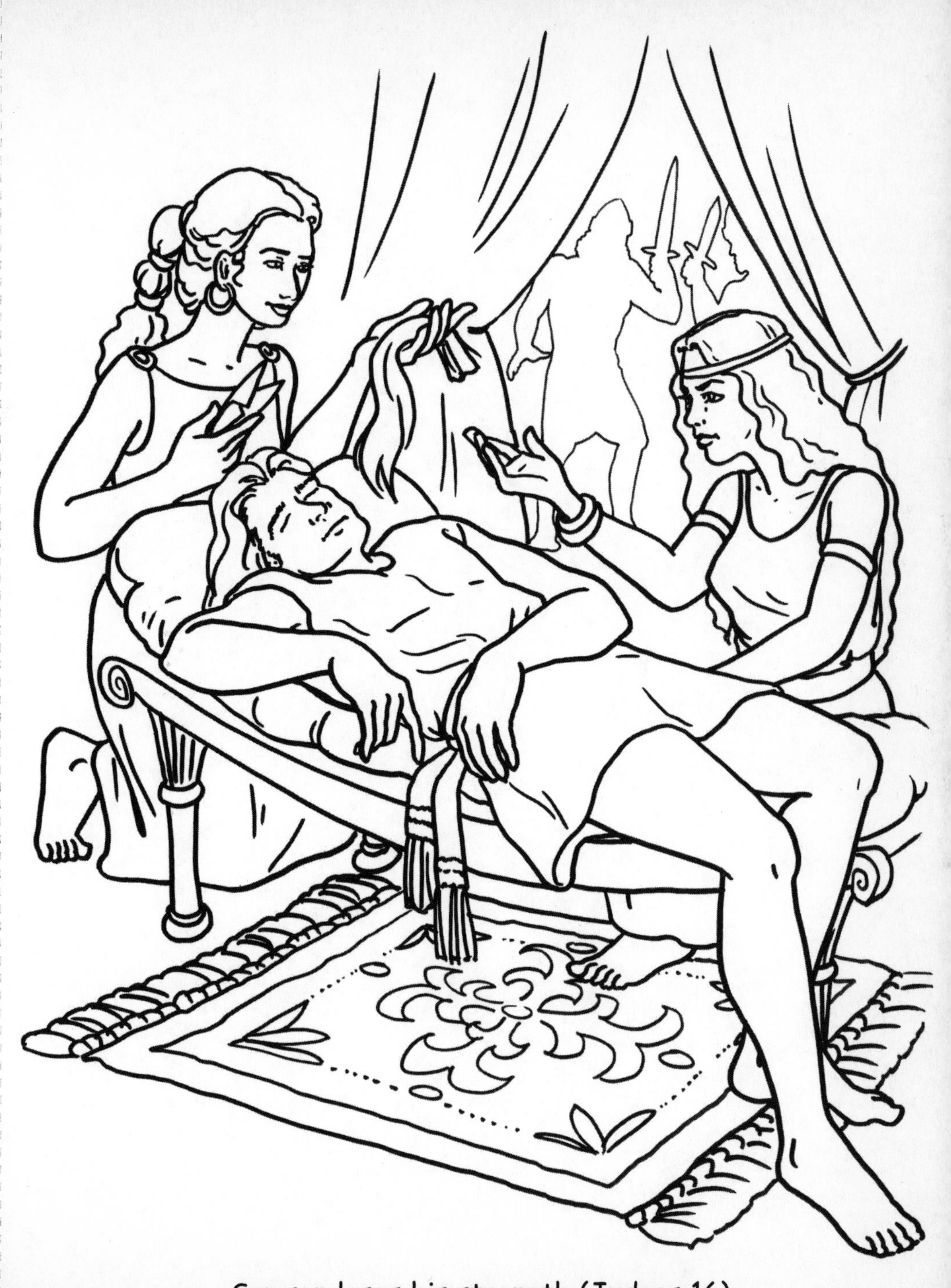

Samson loses his strength (Judges 16)

Samson's death in the temple (Judges 16)

Naomi and Ruth (Ruth 1)

The love story of Ruth and Boaz (Ruth 2-4)

The good man Job (Job)

Jonan and the big fish (Jonah)

The boy Samuel listens to God (1 Samuel 3)

Samuel and Saul (1 Samuel 9–10)

David and Goliath (1 Samuel 17)

Special friends—David and Jonathan (1 Samuel 18–20)

David becomes king (2 Samuel 1–5)

The temple is built (1 Kings 6-8)

Wise king Solomon and the baby (1 Kings 3)

Elijah and the ravens (1 Kings 17)

Elijah and the widow (1 Kings 17)

The contest between God and Baal (1 Kings 18)

Elijah chooses Elisha (1 Kings 19)

Elisha cures a leper (2 Kings 5)

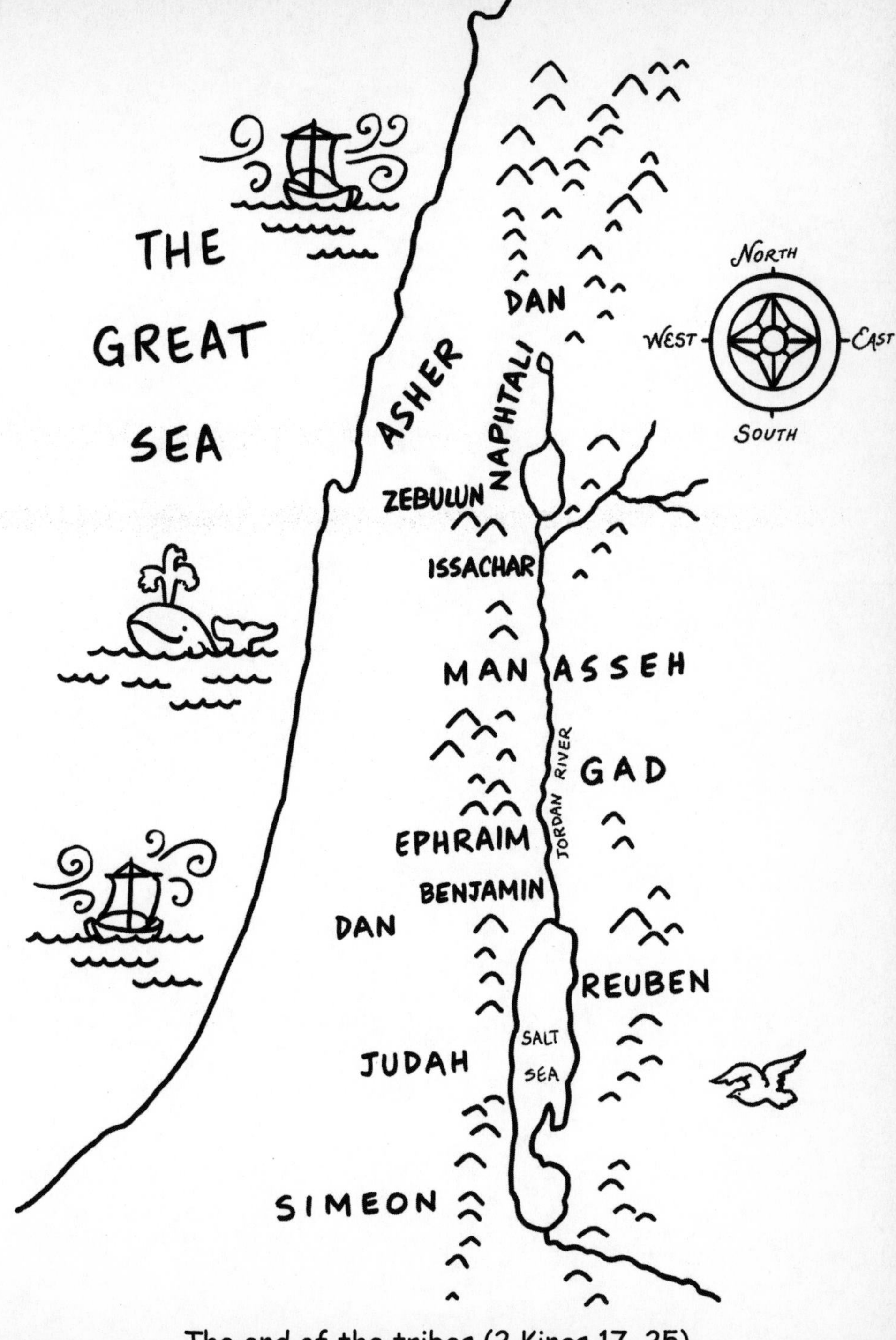

The end of the tribes (2 Kings 17, 25)

Good king Hezekiah (2 Kings 18–20)

Daniel interprets Nebuchadnezzar's dream (Daniel 2)

The fiery furnace (Daniel 3)

The handwriting on the wall (Daniel 5)

Daniel in the lion's den (Daniel 6)

Rebuilding Jerusalem (Ezra)

Queen Esther saves her people (Esther)

Building the wall (Nehemiah)

An angel visits Mary (Luke 1)

Jesus is born in a stable (Luke 2)

The shepherds (Luke 2)

The wise men (Matthew 2)

The boy Jesus in the temple (Luke 2)

John the Baptist (Luke 3)

The baptism of Jesus (Luke 3)

Jesus' forty days in the wilderness (Luke 4)

Jesus teaches the people (Matthew 5–7)

Jesus changes water into wine (John 2)

Fishers of men (Luke 5)

The woman at the well (John 4)

Faith like a mustard seed (Luke 13)

Jesus calms the storm (Mark 4)

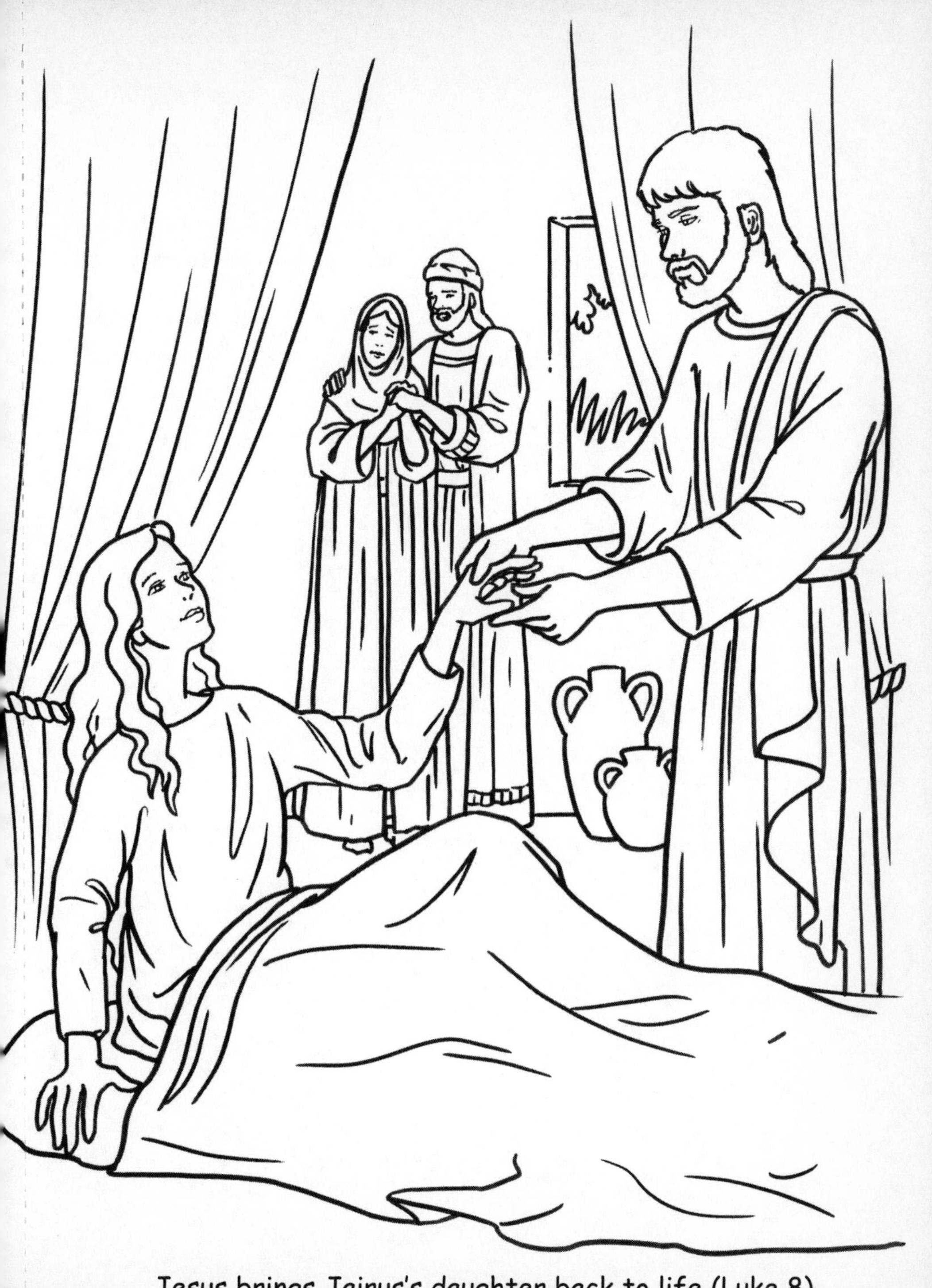

Jesus brings Jairus's daughter back to life (Luke 8)

The loaves and fishes (Luke 9)

Jesus walks on the water (Matthew 14)

Glory on the mountain (Matthew 17)

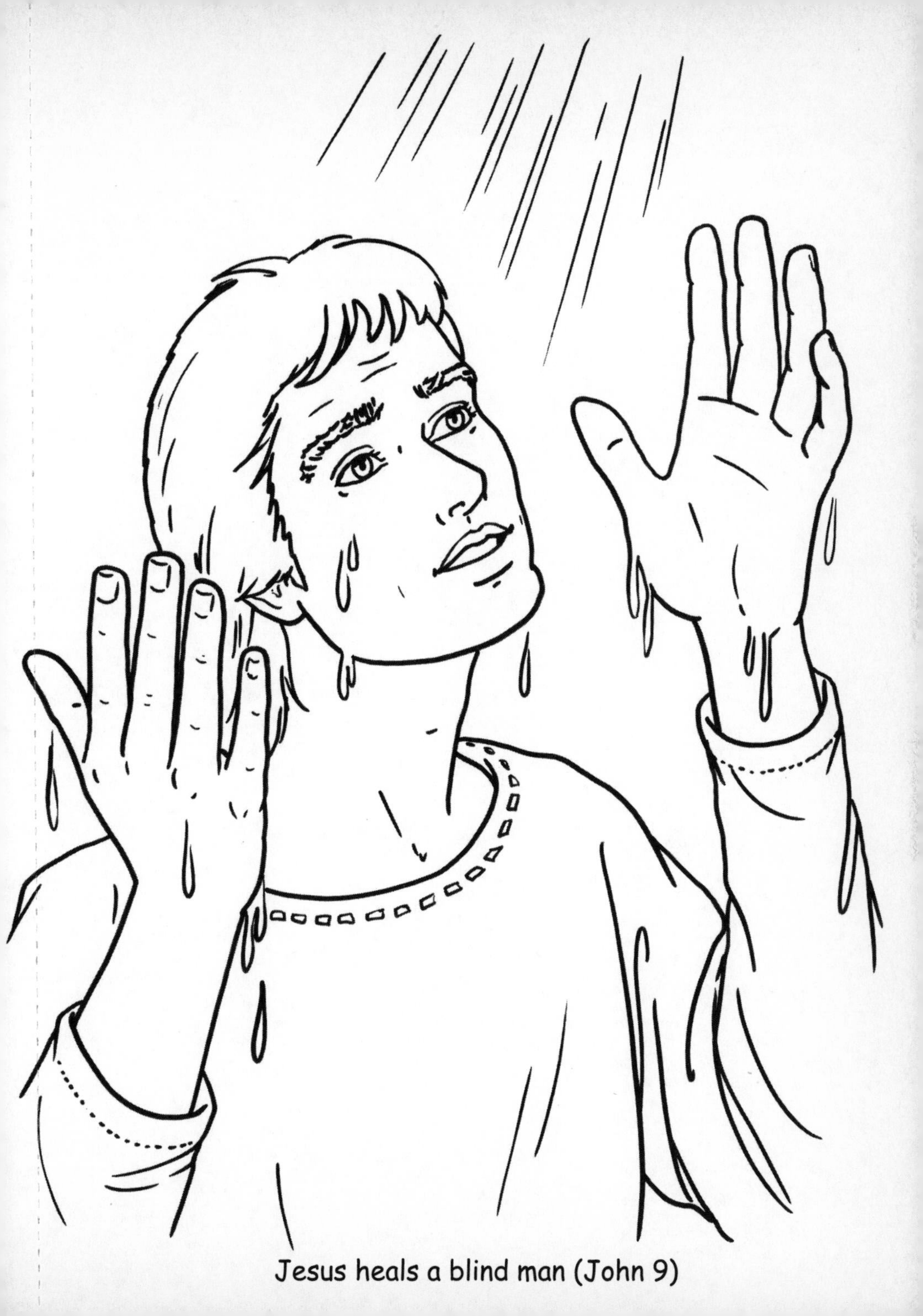

Jesus heals a blind man (John 9)

Jesus raises Lazarus from the dead (John 11)

The parable of the prodigal son (Luke 15)

The parable of the good Samaritan (Luke 10)

Little children come to Jesus (Matthew 19)

Zacchaeus climbs a tree to see Jesus (Luke 19)

Jesus rides into Jerusalem on a donkey (Matthew 21)

Mary's gift to Jesus (John 12)

The Last Supper (Matthew 26)

Jesus prays in the garden of Gethsemane (Matthew 26)

Judas betrays Jesus with a kiss (Matthew 26)

Peter denies Jesus (Matthew 26)

Pilate orders Jesus to be crucified (Matthew 27)

Jesus dies on the Cross (Matthew 27)

The resurrection of Jesus (Matthew 28)

Jesus appears to His disciples (Acts 1)

The Holy Spirit comes at Pentecost (Acts 2)

Peter and John heal a lame beggar (Acts 3)

Philip tells an Ethiopian about Jesus (Acts 8)

Saul becomes a Christian (Acts 9)

Peter has a vision of the gospel for Gentiles (Acts 10)

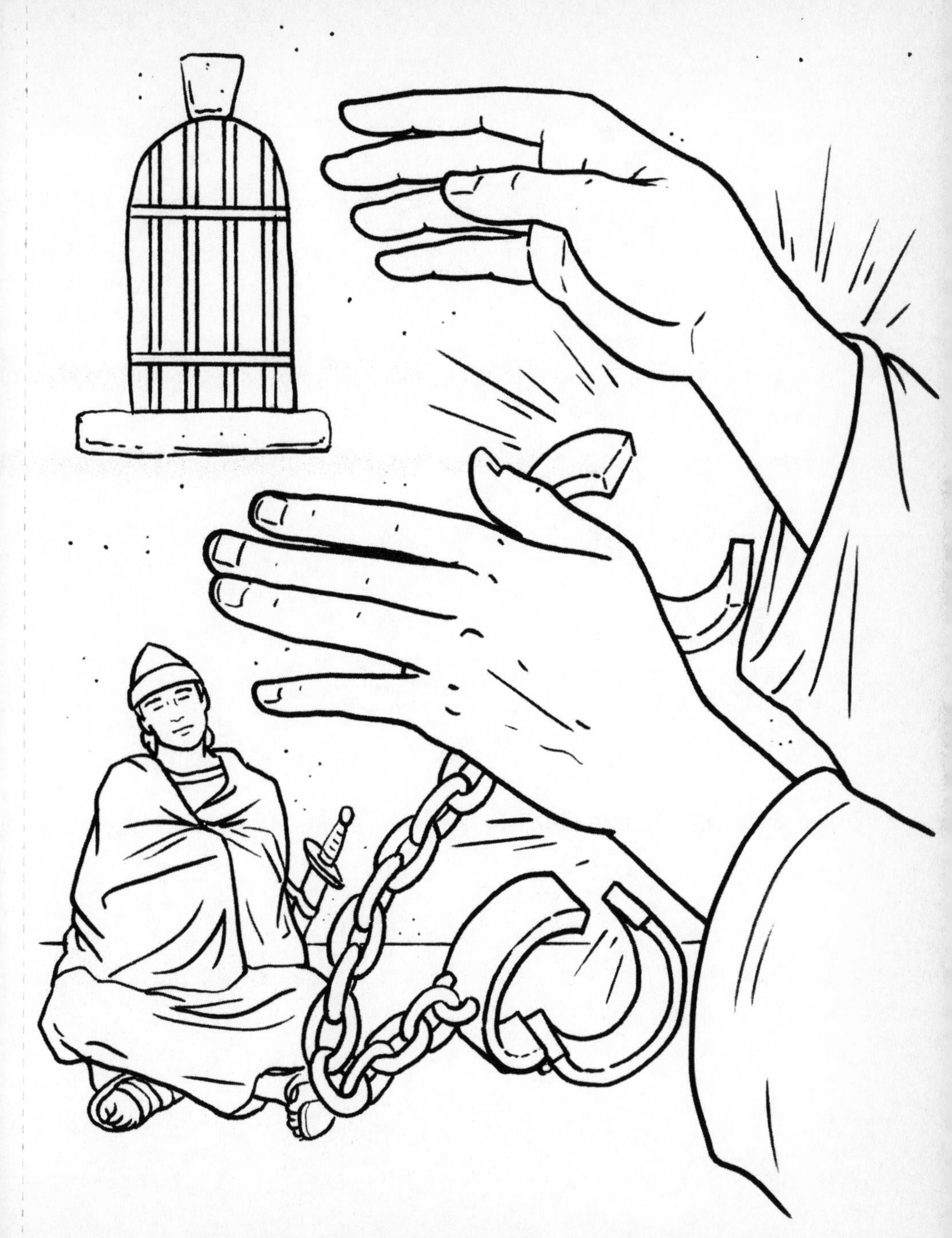

An angel rescues Peter from prison (Acts 12)

Paul faces many dangers to preach the gospel (Acts 27)